Helping the Community

What Do MAIL CARRIERS Do?

Nick Christopher

PowerKiDS press.

New York

Published in 2016 by The Rosen Publishing Group, Inc.
29 East 21st Street, New York, NY 10010

First Edition

Editor: Katie Kawa
Book Design: Katelyn Heinle

Photo Credits: Cover (mail carrier), p. 1 Tetra Images/Getty Images; cover (hands) bymandesigns/Shutterstock.com; back cover Zffoto/Shutterstock.com; p. 5 © iStockphoto.com/BassittART; p. 6 RICHARD HUTCHINGS/ Science Source/Getty Images; pp. 9, 24 (uniform) Kyle Monk/Blend Images/Getty Images; p. 10 (top) © iStockphoto.com/carterdayne; p. 10 (bottom) Migdale Lawrence/Science Source/Getty Images; p. 13 Tupungato/Shutterstock.com; pp. 14, 24 (post office) http://upload.wikimedia.org/wikipedia/commons/d/ d8/LongPointStationHouston.JPG; p. 17 Monkey Business Images/Shutterstock.com; p. 18 mjay/Shutterstock.com; p. 21 William Thomas Cain/Getty Images News/Getty Images; p. 22 © iStockphoto.com/Juanmonino.

Library of Congress Cataloging-in-Publication Data

Christopher, Nick.
 What do mail carriers do? / Nick Christopher.
    pages cm. — (Helping the community)
 Includes bibliographical references and index.
 ISBN 978-1-4994-0650-4 (pbk.)
 ISBN 978-1-4994-0651-1 (6 pack)
 ISBN 978-1-4994-0653-5 (library binding)
 1. Letter carriers—Juvenile literature. I. Title.
 HE6241.C47 2016
 383'.1023—dc23
                                                2015000447

Manufactured in the United States of America

CPSIA Compliance Information: Batch #WS15PK: For Further Information contact Rosen Publishing, New York, New York at 1-800-237-9932

CONTENTS

Mail carriers bring us mail.

Mail carriers also take the mail we want to send to other people.

Mail carriers wear special clothes. This is called a **uniform**.

Mail carriers work in big cities. They work in small towns, too.

Some mail carriers drive a mail truck. It is red, white, and blue.

We Deliver For You.

www.usps.com

People can bring letters to a **post office**. Then, mail carriers deliver those letters.

Mail carriers use a big bag to carry mail.

Mail carriers put letters in people's mailboxes.

Mail carriers bring boxes, too.
Sometimes the boxes have
gifts inside!

Do you like to get mail?

WORDS TO KNOW

post office

uniform

INDEX

WEBSITES

Due to the changing nature of Internet links, PowerKids Press has developed an online list of websites related to the subject of this book. This site is updated regularly. Please use this link to access the list: www.powerkidslinks.com/htc/mail